Muhammad ALI

Boxing Legend

by Gregory N. Peters

CAPSTONE PRESS
a capstone imprint

Trailblazers is published by Capstone Press,
1710 Roe Crest Drive, North Mankato, Minnesota 56003
www.capstonepub.com

Library of Congress Cataloging-in-Publication Data
Peters, Gregory N.
Muhammad Ali boxing legend / By Gregory N. Peters.
pages cm. — (Trailblazers. Sports and Recreation)
Includes bibliographical references and index.
Summary: "Describes the life of boxer Muhammad Ali, from birth to world
champion"—Provided by publisher.
ISBN 978-1-4765-8439-3 (library binding)
1. Ali, Muhammad, 1942—Juvenile literature. 2. Boxers (Sports)—United
States—Biography—Juvenile literature. 3. Role models—Juvenile
literature. I. Title.

GV1132.A4P47 2014
796.83092—dc23   2013030177

Editorial Credits
Christine Peterson, editor; Gene Bentdahl, designer; Eric Gohl, media
researcher; Eric Manske, production specialist

Photo Credits
Alamy: Pictorial Press Ltd, 4; AP Photo: 7, 9, 12–13, 14, 19, 21, 23, 24–25, 32,
H.B. Littell, 10, Mitsunori Chigita, 26, Sal Veder, 16; Newscom: KRT/Eliot J.
Schechter, 37, Mirrorpix, 29, Mirrorpix/Monte Fresco, 30, 34, Olivier Douliery,
40, Reuters/Radu Sigheti, 39, WENN Photos/PF1, cover

Printed in China by Nordica.
1013/CA21301911
029013   007739NORDS14

TABLE OF CONTENTS

Cassius Clay gives his mother a kiss outside their home in Louisville, Kentucky.

CHAPTER 1

Humble Beginnings

On January 17, 1942, a boy was born in Louisville, Kentucky. His parents were Cassius and Odessa Clay. The baby was Cassius Marcellus Clay Jr. One day he would become known as Muhammad Ali.

The Clays lived in a middle-class area of Louisville. Most of their neighbors were African-Americans. Not many white people lived around there. At this time, **segregation** was legal.

Life was hard for many African-Americans. Many faced **discrimination**. There were things they were not allowed to do because of their skin color. So Cassius grew up with many challenges. His life wasn't really going anywhere. But then he met a new friend who changed his life forever.

segregation – the practice of keeping groups of people apart, especially based on race

discrimination – treating people unfairly because of their race, country of birth, or gender

The Stolen Bike

It was 1954. Clay was 12 years old. He decided to go to a meeting at the Louisville Service Club. He had just gotten a new red and white bike. After the meeting he went outside. His bike was gone. He was very upset. Someone came to help him. They went to a nearby boxing gym. A police officer named Joe Martin was in charge that night. He asked Clay about his bike. Clay was angry and said he wanted to fight the thief. Officer Martin asked Clay if he knew how to fight. He invited Clay to learn how. Soon Clay began to train at the gym.

Cassius Clay, age 12

The Star Rises

Joe Martin was Cassius Clay's first trainer. Clay had other trainers too. They helped him become one of the best young boxers. Clay had a very good **amateur** record. Amateurs compete against other amateurs. They do not get paid. Clay fought more than 100 amateur fights. He lost only five. He entered many types of **tournaments**. Clay was the champion many times. He won the Kentucky Golden Gloves tournament six times. He won the Chicago Golden Gloves tournament twice. But that wasn't all. He won the Amateur Athletic Union national tournament. Clay was a **light-heavyweight** at this time. He was 6 feet 3 inches (191 cm) tall. He weighed more than 170 pounds (77 kg).

amateur – describes a sports league that athletes take part in for experience rather than for money

tournament – a series of matches between several players or teams, ending in one winner

light-heavyweight – a boxer weighing up to 175 pounds (79 kg)

Cassius Clay (left) in 1959, trained hard to become a better boxer.

Cassius Clay punches Argentinian fighter Alex Mitoff. Clay won the fight in the sixth round.

Olympics – a competition of many sports events held every four years in a different country; people from around the world compete against each other

heavyweight – a boxer weighing more than 175 pounds (79 kg)

CHAPTER 2

Early Career

All the training paid off. Clay was well known. But he was still an amateur boxer. His next big chance was in the 1960 Summer **Olympics** in Rome, Italy. Clay fought four matches against different fighters. He knocked one out. He won the other three fights by scoring more points than the other fighter. He won the light-heavyweight gold medal. Was this enough? Not for Clay! He wanted to become the **heavyweight** champion. To do this he would have to get a little heavier. He also would have to become a professional.

In 1960 a group of business leaders signed a contract with Clay. He was now a professional boxer. The leaders agreed to pay for his training and help set up boxing matches. For three years Clay fought. By 1964 he had won 19 professional fights. He didn't lose a single one. This gave him a chance to fight Sonny Liston. Liston was the heavyweight champion of the world. Clay's dream was close to coming true.

Clay lands a solid punch against Liston in the third round.

Heavyweight Champion of the World

Clay was bigger now. He had become one of the best. Still, no one thought he could win. Liston was known as the "Big Bear." He was known for his size and power. But his hands and feet were not very fast. Liston's power was what made him scary.

Clay now had a lot of experience. He was bigger now as a heavyweight. He was also fast. The match was set for February 25, 1964. It was Clay's speed against Liston's power. Clay was sure he could win. He said he would win by knockout. He even called Liston a big, ugly bear. The match went as Clay thought it would. It was over when Liston refused to continue fighting which, resulted in a **technical knockout**, or TKO. Clay was excited. He ran to the middle of the ring and yelled, "I'm the greatest!"

technical knockout - a result in boxing when one fighter does not continue to fight

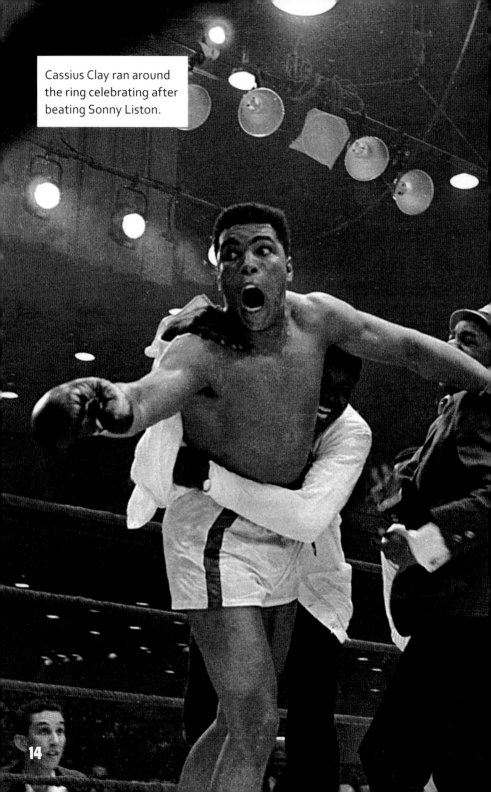

Cassius Clay ran around the ring celebrating after beating Sonny Liston.

I Hear You Loud and Clear

Clay was now the heavyweight champion. He had surprised everyone. Clay was not only fast and strong. He was also loud! The way he spoke to Liston got everyone's attention. He didn't just call him a big, ugly bear. He said that Liston was too ugly to be the world champion. After he won he told all the people who hadn't believed in him to eat their words. Clay wanted everyone to know he was the best.

Before the fight with Liston, Clay made many big claims. One of them became very famous. Clay said he would "float like a butterfly" and "sting like a bee." Clay's fast feet had helped him float away from Liston's punches. His own punches had stung Liston. When Liston didn't get up for Round 7, Clay knew he had been right. He ran around the ring, yelling, "I shook up the world!"

Muhammad Ali announced his new name and religion

CHAPTER 3

The World Champion

Clay was on top of the world! He had beat Sonny Liston. His fancy boxing style impressed the fans. His bold words had caught the world's attention. Who was this man? Had he changed the sport of boxing? Where did his success come from? Clay had an unexpected answer.

Clay held a **press conference** with reporters two days after his fight against Liston. He told the world he believed in **Islam**. He was now part of a group called the Nation of Islam led by Elijah Muhammad. Many white Americans called this group the Black Muslims. Clay had another surprise. About one week later, he announced he had a new name. He was no longer Cassius Marcellus Clay Jr. He was now Muhammad Ali.

press conference – an interview given by a public figure to news reporters

Islam – a religion founded in the seventh century by the prophet Muhammad

17

The U.S. Army Calls

Ali enjoyed life as a world champion. But it didn't last for very long. In the 1960s the U.S. military was involved in Vietnam's **civil war**. Many American soldiers were sent there. Thousands died or were wounded. Many people in the United States were against sending American soldiers to Vietnam. But the U.S. Army needed more soldiers. The Army began to **draft** young men. Those who failed to join when drafted could go to jail.

Ali said his religion did not allow him to fight in wars. This caused a problem. The Army said he would not be made to fight. There were other things he could do. But Ali still refused to join. In 1966 he and his lawyers wrote special legal papers to explain why he refused. They hoped the papers would keep him from being drafted. In the meantime, Ali continued to box.

Muhammad Ali and his lawyer enter an Army office to deal with draft papers.

civil war – a war between different sections or parties of the same country or nation

draft – to select young men to serve in the military

19

Ali fought nine times between 1965 and 1967. He won all his fights, seven by knockout. He was still the greatest in the world. In 1967 he lost his legal case. Ali was told he had to join the Army.

Ali agreed to go to the Army's **induction** ceremony for new soldiers. When his name was called, he did not step forward. He refused to be inducted. As a result, Ali's **passport** was taken away. He was stripped of his world champion title. Ali was not allowed to box any more. Ali did not go to jail. Instead, he fought the decision. He was free until the court reviewed the case.

induction – to formally admit someone into a position or place of honor

passport – an official booklet that allows a person to travel to foreign countries

Ali was led out of an Army building after refusing induction.

A Second Chance

Ali did not fight for three and a half years. He finally got another chance in 1970. The Supreme Court ruled that he did not have to join the Army. Ali could box again.

On October 26, 1970, Ali started his comeback. He defeated Jerry Quarry. This was not a championship fight. But this win helped him get more boxing matches. In 1971 Ali fought Joe Frazier. Frazier was a great fighter. He was became the world champion when Ali was not allowed to box. If Ali beat Frazier, he would be champion again.

The fight took place in Madison Square Garden in New York City. Many big stars were there to see the "Fight of the Century." Ali fought hard. Frazier fought hard too. After 15 rounds the fight was over. The judges all agreed Frazier had won.

Ali was knocked down by Frazier in the 15th round.

Ali kept fighting. He won 12 of his next 13 fights. This earned him another chance to beat Frazier. But Frazier wasn't the world champion anymore. He had lost that title to George Foreman in 1973. But Frazier was still the North American Boxing Federation champion. This was still a big fight for Ali. Winning would give him a chance to regain the world title.

Ali beat Frazier this time. He was now ready to challenge Foreman for the world championship. The match was held October 30, 1974, in Zaire, Africa. The fight was called "The Rumble in the Jungle." The champion was very strong and powerful. He was younger than Ali. He was known for his knockouts. Many thought that Ali's speed would be no match for Foreman's power.

Ali, left, used his "rope-a-dope" strategy to tire George Foreman out.

Again, Ali proved them all wrong. He wore out his opponent by using a **strategy** called "rope-a-dope." His plan was to let Foreman tire himself out. Ali used the sides of the ring for help. Whenever Foreman tried to hit him, Ali leaned back against the ropes and ducked. Ali was still strong in the eighth round. Foreman was tired and weak. Ali won by knockout in that round and became world champion. Once again, Ali was "the greatest."

strategy – a plan for winning

Ali hits Joe Frazier hard during their fight in Manila.

Ali's Team

Angelo Dundee—boxing trainer for almost all of Ali's fights

Drew Bundini Brown—assistant trainer and corner man for Muhammad Ali

CHAPTER 4

The Greatest

The "Thrilla in Manila"

There was no doubt Ali was a great boxer. His first professional loss was to Joe Frazier in 1971. Ali did not get knocked out. Frazier won by getting more points. In their second match, Ali won. This time Ali won more points from the judges. No one really disagreed with these outcomes. Still, there was a question. Who was the better fighter? Frazier or Ali? The first two fights were fierce battles. Everyone expected the third fight to be just as exciting.

The fight took place in 1975, near the city of Manila in the Philippines. It was called the "Thrilla in Manila." People all over the world watched the fight on TV. Ali seemed sure he would win. He called Frazier an ugly, dumb gorilla. But Frazier trained very hard to win. The fight was very tough. One time, Frazier's mouthpiece flew into the crowd. By the end of the 14th round, Frazier's eyes were almost swollen shut. Frazier's trainer stopped the fight. Ali had won! After the fight, Ali praised Frazier. "Joe Frazier is the greatest fighter of all time next to me."

The Unstoppable Champ

Ali had fought many fighters. He had rematches against some. Rematches give fighters a chance to prove they didn't win just by luck. He had fought Sonny Liston and Jerry Quarry twice. He also fought Floyd Patterson, Joe Bugner, and George Chuvalo twice each. He fought Joe Frazier three times. Ken Norton was another fighter Ali fought more than once. In fact, they fought three times. These were some of the hardest fights in Ali's career.

The first match in 1973 lasted for all 12 rounds. Both men landed a lot of strong punches. Norton broke Ali's jaw early in the match. But Ali did not quit. Norton won the match by a **split decision**. At least one judge thought Ali had won. But Norton won the most points, so he won the match.

Muhammad Ali fights Joe Bugner

split decision – a result in boxing when two out of three judges give one fighter more points

Muhammad Ali faces Ken Norton before their third match.

The two boxers fought again six months later. Once again, the fight lasted all 12 rounds. This time Ali won. But it was another split decision. Who was better? The world would have to wait three more years for an answer.

Norton was not afraid of Ali. Both of their matches had been close. Many sports fans thought Ali had lost both fights. Even Ali knew Norton could win. After their second match he said, "Norton is a better fighter than any other fighter I've fought except maybe Frazier."

The third match took place in 1976. It attracted a lot of attention. The match lasted 15 rounds. Many people hoped there would be a knockout. A knockout might make it clear who was the better fighter. But there was no knockout. Ali won by **unanimous decision**. For most people, there was still doubt about which fighter was the best.

unanimous decision - a situation in which all three boxing judges agree on a winner

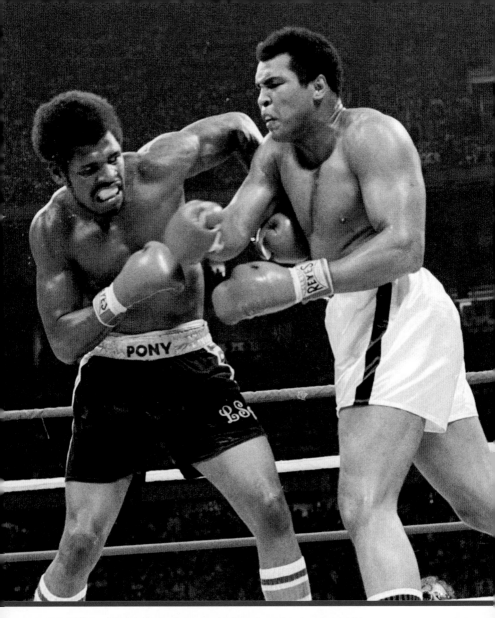

Ali fights Leon Spinks to win his third world championship.

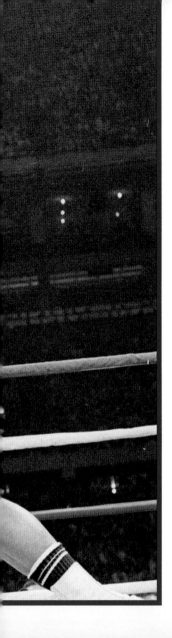

The Third Time Around!

Ali won two more fights after he beat Norton. He did not win either one with a knockout. Some people thought Ali was losing his edge.

Ali was still the world champion when he fought Leon Spinks. Spinks had won the Olympic gold medal in 1976. On February 15, 1978, they met in Las Vegas, Nevada. It was a real battle. The fight lasted all 15 rounds. It ended in a split decision. Ali had lost the world championship for the second time. Some people said Ali took Spinks too lightly.

Spinks decided to give Ali another chance. The two met again on September 15, 1978. This fight was not as close as the first. Ali won by unanimous decision. This made him the first man in history to win the world championship three times. No one could doubt that he was the greatest of all time.

Muhammad Ali warms up before his 1980 fight with Larry Holmes.

CHAPTER 5

After the Bell

Ali fought two more times. In 1980 he was beaten by Larry Holmes. He also fought Trevor Berbick in 1981. He lost that fight too. Ali decided to **retire**. It was clear that his boxing days were over. Three years later he surprised the world. He told everyone he had **Parkinson's disease**. This disease causes tremors, or shakes, in people. Some people think that boxing caused this damage. Doctors aren't sure.

Ali did not let his disease stop him from helping people. In 1997 he helped open the Muhammad Ali Parkinson Center. It offers support for those who have the disease.

---

retire - to give up a line of work

Parkinson's disease - an illness of the brain that causes shaking, slowness, and difficulty with balance

Ali's Public Life

Ali was a hero to many people. He fought against the draft. He fought for his beliefs. He worked for peace. He was one of the greatest boxers of all time.

He worked to help others who had Parkinson's disease. He helped people with illnesses and injuries to compete in sports. In 1996 he lit the torch for the Summer Olympics in Atlanta, Georgia. In 1999 he got another award. *Sports Illustrated* magazine named him the "Sportsman of the Century."

Muhammad Ali holds the torch during the Summer Olympics in Atlanta, Georgia.

Ali also worked hard to help the poor. He went to countries such as Mexico and Morocco. He tried to help the poor there. He also went to Iraq in 1990. This country was ruled by a **dictator**. Ali helped get 14 **hostages** released. The **United Nations** (UN) noticed Ali's work in these countries. In 1998 the UN gave Ali a special title. He was now called a "Messenger of Peace." In many ways, Ali was still "the greatest."

In 2002 Ali visited an Afghanistan bakery run by the UN.

dictator – someone who has complete control of a country, often ruling it unjustly

hostage – a person held against his or her will

United Nations – a group of countries that works together for peace and security

Muhammad Ali stands with his wife, Yolanda, after receiving the Medal of Freedom from President George W. Bush.

A Presidential Citizen

Ali is well known for his good deeds. In 2005 U.S. President George W. Bush gave him the Medal of Freedom. This award honors brave U.S. **citizens**. In 2012 Ali received the **Liberty** Medal. This award is given to people who fight for liberty. Ali did many other things to help people. He wanted them to have a good life too.

Ali turned 70 years old in 2012. Despite his health problems, he has not stopped helping others. He was asked to carry the U.S. flag in the 2012 Summer Olympics in London, England. He had too much trouble walking to carry the flag. But his wife helped him to be there. Ali will always be a hero in many ways.

citizen – a member of a country or state who has the right to live there
liberty – freedom from restriction or control

Muhammad Ali's World Title Fights

Date	Opponent	Result
February 25, 1964	Sonny Liston	W-TKO
May 25, 1965	Sonny Liston	W-KO
November 22, 1965	Floyd Patterson	W-TKO
March 29, 1966	George Chuvalo	W-UD
May 21, 1966	Henry Cooper	W-TKO
August 6, 1966	Brian London	W-KO
September 10, 1966	Karl Mildenberger	W-TKO
November 14, 1966	Cleveland Williams	W-TKO
February 6, 1967	Ernie Terrell	W-UD
March 22, 1967	Zora Folley	W-KO
March 8, 1971	Joe Frazier	L-UD
October 30, 1974	George Foreman	W-KO
March 24, 1975	Chuck Wepner	W-TKO
May 16, 1975	Ron Lyle	W-TKO
June 30, 1975	Joe Bugner	W-UD

Date	Opponent	Result
October 1, 1975	Joe Frazier	W-TKO
February 20, 1976	Jean-Pierre Coopman	W-KO
April 30, 1976	Jimmy Young	W-UD
May 24, 1976	Richard Dunn	W-TKO
September 28, 1976	Ken Norton	W-UD
May 16, 1977	Alfredo Evangelista	W-UD
September 29, 1977	Earnie Shavers	W-UD
February 15, 1978	Leon Spinks	L-SD
September 15, 1978	Leon Spinks	W-UD
October 2, 1980	Larry Holmes	L-TKO

Legend

W – win

L – loss

UD – unanimous decision

SD – split decision

KO – knockout

TKO – technical knockout

Read More

Adler, David A. *Joe Louis: America's Fighter.* Orlando, Fla.: Gulliver Books: Harcourt, 2005.

Burgan, Michael. *Muhammad Ali: American Champion.* Graphic Biographies. Mankato, Minn.: Capstone Press, 2008.

Miller, Davis. *Float and Sting!: One Round with Muhammad Ali.* Graphic Flash. Minneapolis: Stone Arch Books, 2010.

Peña, Matt de la. *A Nation's Hope: The Story of Boxing Legend Joe Louis.* New York: Dial Books for Young Readers, 2011.

Bibliography

pp. 12–13 • "I'm the greatest" http://news.bbc.co.uk/sport2/hi/boxing/3516241.stm

pp. 14–15 • "float like a butterfly" "sting like a bee" http://www.nytimes.com/books/98/10/25/specials/ali-upset.html

pp. 14–15 • "I shook up the world" http://news.bbc.co.uk/sport2/hi/boxing/3516241.stm

pp. 26–27 • "Joe Frazier is the greatest fighter..." http://www.espn.co.uk/boxing/sport/story/120516.html

pp. 30–31 • "Norton is a better fighter..." as quoted in the Montreal Gazette, September 12, 1973: http://news.google.com/newspapers?nid=1946&dat=19730912&id=ck8xAAAAIBAJ&sjid=26EFAAAAIBAJ&pg=3010,3011602

Internet Sites

FactHound offers a safe, fun way to find Internet sites related to this book. All of the sites on FactHound have been researched by our staff.

Here's all you do:
Visit *www.facthound.com*
Type in this code: 9781476584393

 **Super-cool stuff!** Check out projects, games and lots more at
www.capstonekids.com

Titles in this set:

The Best of College Basketball

Muhammad Ali Boxing Legend

The Negro Leagues

Serena and Venus Williams Tennis Stars

Glossary

amateur (AM-uh-chur) • describes a sports league that athletes take part in for experience rather than for money

citizen (SI-tuh-zuhn) • a member of a country or state who has the right to live there

civil war (SIV-il WOR) • a war between different sections or parties of the same country or nation

dictator (DIK-tay-tuhr) • someone who has complete control of a country, often ruling it unjustly

discrimination (dis-kri-muh-NAY-shuhn) • treating people unfairly because of their race, country of birth, or gender

draft (DRAFT) • to select young men to serve in the military

heavyweight (HEV-ee-wate) • a boxer weighing more than 175 pounds (79 kg)

hostage (HOSS-tij) • a person held against his or her will

induction (in-DUHKT-shuhn) • to formally admit someone into a position or place of honor

Islam (ISS-luhm) • a religion founded in the seventh century by the prophet Muhammad

liberty (LIB-ur-tee) • freedom from restriction or control

light-heavyweight (LITE HEV-ee-weyt) • a boxer weighing up to 175 pounds (79 kg)

Olympics (oh-LIM-piks) • a competition of many sports events held every four years in a different country; people from around the world compete against each other

Parkinson's disease (PAR-kin-suhnz duh-ZEEZ) • an illness of the brain that causes shaking, slowness, stiffness, and difficulty with balance

passport (PASS-port) • an official booklet that proves that a person is a citizen of a certain country; passports allow people to travel to foreign countries

press conference (PRESS KAHN-fuhr-uhns) • an interview given by a public figure to news reporters

retire (ri-TIRE) • to give up a line of work

segregation (seg-ruh-GAY-shuhn) • the practice of keeping groups of people apart, especially based on race

split decision (SPLIT de-SIZH-uhn) • a result in boxing when two out of three judges give one fighter more points

strategy (STRAT-uh-jee) • a plan for winning

technical knockout (TEK-nuh-kuhl NOK-out) • a result in boxing when one fighter does not continue to fight

tournament (TUR-nuh-muhnt) • a series of matches between several players or teams, ending in one winner

unanimous decision (yoo-NAN-uh-muhss di-SIZH-uhn) • a situation in which all three boxing judges agree on a winner

United Nations (yoo-NI-ted NAY-shuns) • a group of countries that works together for peace and security

Index